INITIATING TONGUES AT THE POINT OF TEMPTATION

Praying in the SPIRIT WORKS!!!

Andre' LaFlora

Herald Acoustic Energies

www.reverendwho.com

Initiating Tongues at the Point of Temptation

Contents

Acknowledgements

For the last forty years, I have done my music business using my middle name, recognizing my good friend Andrae Crouch. This project falls more to the pastoral, ministerial side, so I have included my first name Thomas, in honor of two of the greatest, most honorable men I know. My father and I looked at a letter appointing my grandfather Superintendent Thomas LeFlore Sr as a church pastor in January 1927. He was a Church of God in Christ District Superintendent in Arkansas for over fifty years. From my memories of him, without a doubt a holy man of God, trying to be like Jesus. One day when I was a teenager napping in a chair by the front door, someone knocked at the door. He answered the front door,.. "whom seek ye" (Laughs!). And of course his wife Mother Pearl...the tiny general! Next, there is my father Superintendent Thomas LaFlora Jr, founder and Senior pastor of Unity Church Of God In Christ, Memphis Tennessee where I pastor now.   He has been on ordination boards for 50 years, for two COGIC presiding Bishops in Memphis Tennessee , and been chairman 39 of those years. He is STILL my instructor.   His wife, my mother, District Missionary Virgie M. LaFlora, who to this day has been my biggest supporter.   My uncle Bishop Samuel Smith and State Mother Lee Ella Smith, because of their friendship with Bishop and Mother Benjamin and Catherine Crouch gave the opportunity to come to know Andrae.   Another uncle Superintendent Henry A. Spight and my second mom State Mother Zelma Spight, gave me much counsel in my early walk with the Lord.   My brother Pastor Lenoir P. and wife Idell LaFlora Sr and the House of Praise virtual ministries, my first partner in "the Great Commission Conquest."   Bishop G.E. Patterson who ordained me and Bishop

Jerry L. Maynard who appointed me pastor, I appreciate them.   Among countless others I could call, I thank them all for their righteous legacies ,prayers and influence on my life. Of course, Thank you Unity!

Foreword

This is SPIRITUAL BUSINESS, that does not register with the carnal mind (Romans 8:6-8). A carnal minded person thinks you are crazy with that spiritual stuff. Meanwhile, you don't take depression medication, smoke cannabis, drink or do drugs because you have Peace…in Christ, and

 if something is bothering you, you know where to find peace. Hey…Christ offers this to everybody!! The question is, Do YOU have the "Gift of Faith" to believe?

   Truth is, if you have asked God to forgive your sins and have asked Him for the gift of the Holy Ghost, with your sincere mind aimed Godward, you can moan to Him or initiate speaking in Tongues regarding any concern, or just to worship Him…and He will take over that prayer session "In The Spirit", uplift your mind, give you victory at the point of temptation and deal with any situations you are facing the way He knows is best. Attack all of your anxieties and mental battles in Tongues and let His Spirit do the praying!   All of this is available by FAITH in Christ!!!   Have Peace!

(PS: You can Whisper in tongues, He still hears you!!)

www.reverendwho.com
the1.revwho@gmail.com

Initiating Tongues at the Point of Temptation

To pray in Tongues is another level of faith, a Higher level of faith, especially when you initiate the tongues. You have to bring the Holy Ghost from the peak of a firey hot church service home to your point of temptation,.. home to your real battle! Now its Winning Time!!!   -TAL

Chapter 1

Spiritual Business

In the eyes and minds of the world, the things we will discuss in this book are foolish. According to 1 Corinthians 1:18- 29, we find that God chooses to use things people call foolish to confound the "smart" people.   It is a shame to be so smart, yet the same smartness that should bring a ship successfully to its destination causes it to sink. This is what happens when one has too much sense, or is too smart to accept God's love invitation.   With that thought in mind…. Give me the foolishness.

This discussion is about Spiritual Business, and falls into the realm of Divine Realities, which is frankly…God's Business. In this realm, human reasoning has no authority.   Divine Realities are not bound by your reasoning, your logic, your opinion, your mathematics, your science, your training or what you think you know. It is above your mental and physical pay grades. After all, you have only been alive a few minutes and will be gone in a few minutes. But if you can yield to God's truth believing that Jesus Christ is God's Son and that He died so that your soul wouldn't have to because of your sins, and rose for your justification, you can and will live spiritually forever! Yes, these are spiritual facts that apply to everyone that has ever lived and must be address by each person. Only the people with the "gift of faith" to believe this can accept it. We have testimonies of people that have experienced existence after death. It is no fairy tale. Hallelujah for the wonderful future of believers that accept God's love offer!!

To not be aware of the spiritual realities is not uncommon. In John the third chapter, Nicodemas was highly educated in Judaism and a Pharisee, well trained in Judaic law of the Holy

Scriptures.   Yet when Jesus introduced the spiritual reality for the need of every man to be born again, he had never heard of such. It is possible today many clergy don't know of the full benefits of living life "In The Spirit".   And if they don't know they can't tell you.

Many people that attend church every week, some have lived their whole lives failing to realize the depth of the spiritual side of church life.   The fact is, it is a spiritual place by nature and not just a social gathering.   Many have no idea what their spiritual make up is, how much of themselves is spiritual, the need for that spiritual part of them to be fed daily (not just weekly), and then the outflow of imparting into others. They have heard about heaven and hell and that everyone will go to one or the other forever, but haven't grasped the truth that relationship with Jesus Christ "in the Spirit" is profitable mentally, physically, financially, relationally in this world....and then there is eternal heaven.

They live in physical and spiritual worlds. They can see the physical world all around them, but the spiritual is the biggest, It last literally forever, and determines your present mental, physical, financial and relationship wellbeing.

For the best of both worlds, embrace and chase God with these truths we will discuss.

Chapter 2

Levels Of Prayer

Many books have been written about prayer or praying "in the Spirit", that you may have read. Add this one to your collections.

John 4:24 says that "God is a Spirit: and they that worship Him Must worship Him in Spirit and truth." To say our prayers is necessary for basic communication with God and are, for the sake of this discourse, the lower levels of prayer. To pray on this level, one needs to be familiar with the Word of God so that they pray with an understanding (1 Corinthians 14:15). You should read some scripture every day, praying that the Lord opens your mind to His Word.   As you read God's Word, it will reveal to you God's character and help you understand Who you are talking to. It will also show you yourself and help you to know better what to pray to God for.

And for the record, we pray to Jehovah God through Jesus Christ, which is the only existing Deity (John 17:3). Muslims, Hindu, Buddhist and every religion prays to gods that don't exist, which is satan's way of taking attention from the true God.   Jesus made it clear when He said in John 14:5 "I am the way, the truth, and the life: no man cometh unto the Father, but by Me."

In Jesus, there is no longer a need for religion because religion is merely man's search for God. In Christ, God is found.   So this level of prayer is always necessary.   But more is available.   The Luxury of praying "in the Spirit" no religion on earth has!

To let the Spirit of God pray through you are the beginnings of higher levels of prayer.   On these levels burdens are lifted, minds are eased, peace comes with the assurance you are right with God and He is going to bring you out victorious in what ever you are dealing with.

Since God is a Spirit, the best way to pray is "In The Spirit."

Unlike any world religion, praying in the Spirit or praying in the Holy Ghost (Ephesians 6:18; Jude 1:20 KJV) is the prayer session where the Spirit takes over the prayer to the point where it is not you praying, but Him praying through you, or according to Acts 2:4, "giving you the utterance. When the Spirit of God is praying and interceding for you, He is doing it according to the Will of God (Romans 8:26-27), which is the Only Prayer God Answers.   When our prayers are off course, the Holy Spirit never gets it wrong interceding to the father for us. If your desired prayer is not God's will for you, He will reveal it to you.   His will is Always Best for you!   Also, when you pray in tongues, it is your spirit praying on a spiritual level that is above your understanding, covering things that you don't know to include in your prayers...but Need to be covered (1Corinthians 14:14; Romans 8:26).

Praying in the Spirit repairs and uplifts the mind and your mental state like nothing on earth can. When Proverbs 4:23 KJV says "Keep thy heart with all diligence; for out of it are the issues of life."   The New living Translation says it like this: "Guard your heart above all else, for it determines the course of your life. In the Hebrew the heart and the mind are basically the same, so we keep or guard our minds by praying "in the Spirit" OFTEN throughout the day and night.   Also, nothing in the Hebrew definition of the word "issue" is associated with "problem" or "trouble".   So if we read the verse thinking it is talking about problems in life, we are missing the biblically intended meaning.   The Hebrew definition of "issue" has to do with the good your heart or mind can produce. So praying in the Spirit will bring out the Godly best that can come out of us, ultimately the Purpose of God for us, which is our highest created call. You want to keep your mind because "with the mind I serve the law of God (Romans 7:25).

I am here to tell you, the best prayers are the ones where the Spirit takes over because He is lifting your mind and strengthening your body while He flows through you, despite turmoil being all around you. Remove the stagnation in your life as a believer by praying OFTEN "In The Spirit"...Starting NOW! It's a Continual Revival!!

Chapter 3

Instant in Prayer

The person of the Spirit of God, the Holy Ghost is instantly, and presently available. Romans 12:12 tells us to "rejoice in hope; patient in tribulation; continuing INSTANT IN PRAYER! Contrary to popular opinion, it does not take a long time to tap into the Spirit of God.   One does not have to pray for an hour and a half and go into a trance for the Holy Ghost to arrive.   When worship service starts, the praise singers will say "let's usher in the presence of the Lord." Guess what??   The Lord is already there!   The question is....when will you arrive?   We can all agree that when we get to church our minds are often scattered everywhere. It is a matter of us becoming Aware Of HIS Presence.   Psalms 139:7-12 informs us that there exist no place in the universe where God is not there, and that He is present everywhere simultaneously, or at the same time.

As far as praying, Jesus assures us in Matthew 18:20 that "where two or three are gathered together in my name, there am I in the midst of them." Chapter 28:20 He confirms "I am with you always, even unto the end of the world." Since God is everywhere at all times, believers can Enjoy The Presence Of The Lord Anywhere and Anytime. You can be in the Spirit instantaneously if and when your mind is Godward. Always ask God to forgive you just incase you may have sinned at some point, before invoking the Holy Ghost. I have prayed this throughout the day for decades. Be assured, if there is sin in your life, the Holy Spirit WILL bring it to your attention to help you get it out. That is good news because if you really want to please God, you want all sin out. That's another way the Spirit of God helps us.

Acts 2:4 KJV says, "And they were all filled with the Holy Ghost, and began to speak with other tongues, as the Spirit gave them utterance." Observe who began to speak with other tongues.

It was not the Holy Ghost who began to speak. It was the people who were there in the upper room. They opened their mouths and the Spirit gave utterance. Jesus said in John 7:38, "He that believeth on me, as the scripture hath said, out of his belly shall flow rivers of living water." A river does not stop and start. It flows continually. Since He is available everywhere all the time, we can enjoy Him by praying "In the Spirit" instantly...anywhere you are like a flowing river. From personal experience I have found that if I initiate tongues with my sincere mind toward the Lord, toward the throne, even the heart of God, the Holy Ghost immediately joins in and takes over......and I'm LOVING IT!!!

Multiple times a day I enjoy this, driving my car, washing my hands, anytime my mind is momentarily free, God is free to meet me! Amazing! Each experience varies, but it is wonderful to know I can tap into Eternal God anytime, "IN THE SPIRIT", whether my mood is high or low.

Here is the broadness of the God you serve through Jesus Christ: He is not limited to communicating in English, or whatever your language is.   As a matter of fact, you can moan to Him and He understands you perfectly. Romans 8:26 KJV says "..the Spirit itself maketh intercession for us with groanings which cannot be uttered." 2 Corinthians 12:4 mentions "unspeakable words, which it is not lawful for a man to utter." In my opinion, this is why the notion of "hallelujah" being the highest praise is debatable, and hard to believe for me.   It is a lot to assume it has even been revealed to our wicked and adulterous minds (Mat. 16:4; 12:39; Mark 8:38) what God highest praise is, if we have any ideal how unimaginably Big He is.   Let me see if I can spark some thought in your minds.   His real estate holdings cover quindecillions (millions of trillions) of stars and planets.   Psalms 147:4 says "He telleth the number of stars; He calleth them all by their names."

Who knows how many times God has run the same types of scenarios He is running on earth right now, in eternity past. How many other planets and stars is He running similar scenarios right now?... while we're worrying about "telephone disconnected, waiting on the next paycheck and trying to get our next box of chicken?" Let us not be foolishly ego centric. The God we serve is unimaginably big, but He has time for you and longs to commune with you. Psalms 147:3 says "He healeth the broken in heart, and bindeth up their wounds." That same big God understands your heart (Jeremiah 17:10) and interprets your moans. He is not bound by one language. So……

When a believer begins to speak out of their language with a sincere mind Godward...aimed at the throne of God, the Holy Ghost WILL take over and do the praying! Hallelujah!! It does not have to be wild and uncontrolled because 'the spirits are subject to the prophets", and "God IS NOT the author of confusion, but of peace.."(1 Corinthians 14:32,33). It is possible to whisper in tongues.   I certainly do! Anywhere you can give Him that focus, He is present.   What a privilege to be able to pray "in the Spirit" on the operating table, in court, getting robbed (God forbid, but there are testimonies of such!), in the face of trouble, or on a sunny day when you feel good and have plenty of money.   Every believer should pray "in the Spirit" multiple times a day and throughout the night, instant in prayer where ever you are.   There should be no activity that you can't include or welcome the Lord in. No period of time in any day or night where the Lord is not welcome.   If you allow such, the devil will occupy it.   At the movies, watching TV, at work, at school, at fun...where ever you are. His presence is available to raise your mind, lift burdens, give peace, give direction, and confirm your relationship with God.

Know Him "In The Spirit!" If you are clergy, be careful to pray Often "In The Spirit" so that the Lord "knows you In the Spirit" (Matthew 7:22-23). It is not enough to be a preacher, wear collars and robes and do churchy stuff. God had better "know" you..."In The Spirit." Only then will you bear what God calls..."Fruit" (Genesis 4:1; John 15:2-8; 15:16).

Chapter 4

Tongues at the Point of Temptation

[Replacing your sin session with tongues and the Holy Ghost!]

Now I come to the subject on the cover of the book, "Speaking in or initiating Tongues At the point of Temptations".   The first Rule in dealing with besetting sins, weaknesses and the "can't help its" is to NEVER GIVE UP ON GOD UNTIL THE DAY HE DELIVERS YOU!!!   There may be times when you commit the sin again after praying about it.   If you fall and yield to temptation, be informed that God's grace is bigger than any sin you can do, and according to 2 Chronicles 15:2 the Lord is with you as long as you are with Him.   That means He never gives up on you! Ask God to forgive you, give you victory over that sin, and declare to God you will never leave Him and declare you ARE the righteousness of God in the face of that sin until the day you are delivered (2 Corinthians 5:21).

All of this is available By Faith In God!! (Romans 10: 8-10).   You will be delivered as long as you chase God for deliverance!   1 John 1:9 KJV says " If we confess our sins, he is faithful and just to forgive us our sins, and to cleanse us from all unrighteousness."   DON'T EVER LET THE DEVIL, ANYBODY, OR ANY NOTION IN YOUR HEAD,... TALK YOU INTO FORSAKING OR TURNING YOUR BACK ON GOD!!!   In Christ there is always Grace and deliverance for anybody that comes to God for it and wants to please Him.   Our inadequacies are displayed in our human weaknesses.   And where as the first Adam came and disobeyed, giving us all a blood lineage to destruction, the second adam ..."Jesus" lived and obeyed the Father perfectly and gave us a Blood covering of perfection through which God views us and declares us justified!!   Hallelujah!! So even though we pursue perfection all of our lives, we obtain it through Christ perfect life.   Our quest for perfection means arresting all besetting sins,

18

even thoughts, and bringing them under the knowledge of Christ (2 Corinthians 10:5).

Now... let's give you the answer to victory over besetting sins.

We now realize that we have the freedom to initiate the tongues and have the Holy Ghost join us immediately, when our mind is sincere and aimed at the Lord. Once you begin to cultivate and use these truths, you will find that tempting thoughts are arrested immediately and shot down! Hallelujah! There is no question that when you are tempted, you can start speaking in tongues on the spot, aiming "your sincere mind Godward" (it only works in sincerity toward God), and you will experience victory over any and all besetting sins.   This is because you are praying multiple times throughout the day and night "in the Spirit", sitting in Heavenly Places with God in the Spirit.   Whether driving your car in the daytime or lying in bed at three o'clock am, this works.   This brings a change of mind in you.

You can Attack Every Mental Hardship by "Praying In The Spirit", initiating the tongues with your sincere mind aimed at God.   Every mental hardship, every temptation, every anxiety, depression, suicidal thoughts, everything that takes your peace can be subdued by praying "In The Spirit."   God can give you direction concerning your financial needs, or any concerns when you pray OFTEN in the Spirit.

All types of sexual sins and imaginations can be subdued when you Pray OFTEN "IN THE SPIRIT", whether it be pornography, heterosexual adultery, homosexuality, pedophilia, masturbation, bestiality...whatever it is.   Even drugs and foreign substance abuse.   No man made medications can solve the mental problems many people face.   This is spiritual business and the influence of evil spirits on the physical world and people.

 Your WEAPON is Praying In The Holy Ghost Often throughout the day and night.   You can whisper in tongues if you need to!

When ever you are tempted, start speaking in tongues aiming your sincere mind toward God. Do this whenever the thought begins to come into your mind.   Arrest them immediately!   Do not tolerate them!   The more you pray "in the Spirit," the more the pleasure of pleasing God will overcome earthly pleasures as your mind changes feeding on God's Word.

This is a process and it is possible for you to fail sometimes during this period.   But there is no failure in God's forgiveness, so ask Him to forgive you, take the desire for that sin away from you and keep chasing God until you are delivered. DO THIS!...DO THIS!...DO THIS!...and you will enjoy victory over your besetting sins!   THIS IS YOUR WEAPON!!!   Remember...to the blind and unbelieving all of this is foolish, but to those who believe ...it is the Power and Wisdom Of God!! (1 Corinthians 1:23-24; 2:5; Rom.1:16)

Chapter 5

Conclusion

Many believers high and low, from bishops to ushers at the lobby doors, cooks, choir members.....people in church... have their secret sins and problems. Jesus prayed all night then chose twelve men to follow Him.   And all....All...ALL of them had problems and yet...they were God's choice.   Every great man and woman in the Bible had their personal challenges. Only Jesus had none (1 Peter 2:21-22).   The word "infirmity" in the Greek means feebleness of body or mind. When Paul spoke of his infirmities, he did not say illness as most like to assume, so the definition of his concern could have been very broad.   Whatever he was dealing with, Jesus' answer was "My grace is sufficient for thee: for my strength is made perfect in weakness" (2 Corinthians 12: 9-10). Jesus is the only One who brings the believer up to God's standard.

We tap into His perfection and His victory by "praying in the Spirit" as often as we can, realizing that these weaknesses and struggles are spiritual and can only be solved by the Spirit of God working in us. And with the many church sex scandals the body of Christ has encountered that are coming to light now because of human flaws, the message of this book is timely. According to 2 Samuel 12: 14, these scandals "give the enemies of the Lord great occasion to blaspheme." Believers!...don't just pray people....."Pray In The Spirit!!!" "PRAY IN THE HOLY GHOST!!!"

...OFTEN!!!

About the Author

Thomas Andre LaFlora is the pastor of Unity Church Of God In Christ in Memphis, Tennessee.   He is the founder of Herald Records & Acoustic Energies and Love Jam Music (BMI).   He holds a Bachelors of Business Administration from the University of Memphis and Certification of Biblical Studies from Charles Harrison Mason Bible College in Memphis, Tennessee.

See Andre LaFlora music on Facebook and Youtube.
www.reverendwho.com
the1.revwho@gmail.com
atunitycogic.org

Made in the USA
Columbia, SC
22 September 2022

67761003R00020